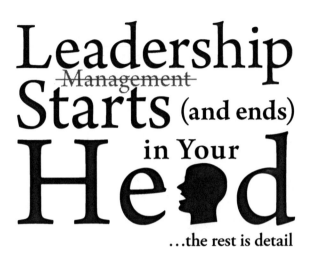

Leadership ~~Management~~ Starts (and ends) in Your Head
...the rest is detail

Bob Dailey

authorHOUSE®

AuthorHouse™
1663 Liberty Drive
Bloomington, IN 47403
www.authorhouse.com
Phone: 1-800-839-8640

© 2014 Bob Dailey. All rights reserved.

No part of this book may be reproduced, stored in a retrieval system, or transmitted by any means without the written permission of the author.

Published by AuthorHouse 10/08/2014

ISBN: 978-1-4969-4454-2 (sc)
ISBN: 978-1-4969-4453-5 (e)

Any people depicted in stock imagery provided by Thinkstock are models, and such images are being used for illustrative purposes only.
Certain stock imagery © Thinkstock.

This book is printed on acid-free paper.

Because of the dynamic nature of the Internet, any web addresses or links contained in this book may have changed since publication and may no longer be valid. The views expressed in this work are solely those of the author and do not necessarily reflect the views of the publisher, and the publisher hereby disclaims any responsibility for them.

To JRD, JRF, JRS,

and BAJ

Contents

Introduction 1

1. You Are Accountable … Period. 3
   - Scrambled Eggs or Omelets? 5
2. The Customer Comes First! 6
   - Becoming the Chief Simplicity Officer 8
3. Employees Don't Work for You 10
   - Theory X and Theory Y 12
4. Maintain Two Standard Deviations 14
   - Moving a Boulder 17
5. Deliver Results 18
   - Chasing Mice 22
6. Don't Ride Your Fender! 23
   - Avoiding Rocks 26
7. The Best Managers Are Curious 27
   - One of the Most Powerful Words in Our Vocabulary: Why? 30
8. Always Cultivate Talent 31
   - The Kung Fu Master 33
9. Don't Treat Everyone the Same 34
   - Encouraging Words 36

10. Never Stop Learning (or Teaching) 37
    – Think like a Teacher 41

11. Match Authority with Responsibility... 42
    – No One Is "Just a ..." 45

12. Visualize Success 46
    – Remembering to Breathe 49

13. You Only Control One Thing... 50
    – Just Another PICNIC 53

14. What Does This All Mean?... 54
    – Searching for Awesomeness 55

Acknowledgments 57

About the Author 59

# Introduction

Whether you manage a department of three employees or an international organization with thousands of employees, one thing impacts your success more than anything else.

When describing how to succeed in the game of baseball, Yogi Berra once said, "90 percent is half mental." Clearly, the secret to success in baseball is the same as leadership ... and just about everything else in life.

It's all in your head. Success is all about *your* mental approach. The rest is detail.

Realizing that it's **not** about you, while focusing solely on creating an environment where others can succeed, is critical to your organization's success. Notice I didn't say *your* success. That's lesson one. Your success happens only as a by-product of helping others and your organization achieve success. Personal success without the success of those around you is empty and should never enter your mind.

This book is divided into bite-sized chapters. It should take about an hour to read. Take some time after each chapter and think about how it applies to what you do in your organization today.

Each chapter provides a guidepost for improving your mental approach and taking your leadership game to new heights.

I purposely left out many of the technical aspects of managing (the detail). Operations management, span of control, strategic and organizational planning, budgeting, managing change, establishing internal controls for risk management, and a host of other how-to items were ignored. These are all-important but pale by comparison to the importance of the mind-set you bring to each of them.

This book will help you understand and embrace the mental side of leadership ... where true leaders spend most of their time.

Let's roll!

-Bob Dailey, June 2014

1. You Are Accountable ... Period.

I remember talking with a friend who had just been promoted to manage a branch operation. Prior to that, he had been a high-producing sales person in the branch for at least six or seven years. I congratulated him on his promotion, and I'll never forget his response.

"Yeah, now I can finally do whatever I want ... come and go as I please."

I couldn't believe what I was hearing. Clearly, he didn't understand that, as a manager, he was as accountable to each employee as each employee was to him. In fact, the manager has a much higher level of accountability than his employees do.

Whether managers realize it or not, and whether they care or not, each of their employees is looking at them as the example. A manager's behavior, habits, and personality traits are all on display. Employees will often mimic their manager's behavior and style. The amazing thing about this truism is that employees will even mimic a manager whose traits they despise.

If my friend decided to "do whatever he wanted and come and go as he pleased," his employees would behave the same way. There are no free passes, especially for managers.

When managers provide opinions or make promises, employees listen and take action. In most organizations, an employee's manager is that employee's only connection to the rest of the organizational structure. The perspectives and priorities that the manager embraces will represent the organization's priorities in the eyes of his or her employees.

The environment that managers create by their actions and behavior will represent the organizational environment to their employees. It doesn't matter if the company has a culture of openness and creativity if a manager has just the opposite mindset. To the employees of a closed-minded manager, the company will "become" closed-minded.

If your direct reports are managers, ensuring that their perspectives and priorities match the organization's priorities is critical. You should spend a significant amount of your time "painting the vista" for your managers and their employees. The vista is the broad view of the organization's objectives and how each employee and department fits and contributes to achieving these objectives.

The manager's job is only to help employees be successful. If the employees aren't successful, the organization will fail. If they succeed, so does the organization. The manager is responsible and accountable for both their successes and their failures.

The weakest managers I've known have ignored this fact. They may view an employee's success as a potential threat (making the manager look less valuable by comparison). This same weak manager will often leave employees twisting in the wind and isolated when they fail … as if the manager had nothing to do with the failure.

As the manager, you are accountable for both successes and failures. You are accountable to each of your employees to help them be successful. You are responsible for understanding how each employee defines success for himself or herself and the organization.

Here's the tricky part. It's your job to take all of your employees' perspectives on success and point them in a direction that creates success for the organization. So, no, you don't get to do whatever you want now that you're a manager.

Scrambled Eggs or Omelets?

Scrambling eggs is easy:

- Whip a couple of eggs in a bowl.
- Pour the mixture in a heated pan, preferably over melted butter.
- Stir randomly until the eggs are cooked.
- Less stirring equals larger egg pieces. More stirring equals smaller egg pieces.
- Enjoy with Cholula.

What about omelets? A little more complicated:

- Determine what you want in your omelet.
- Slice and/or precook (sauté) the filling ingredients.
- Whip a couple of eggs in a bowl.
- Pour the egg mixture in a heated pan.
- Let the egg mixture sit in the pan until mostly cooked.
- Flip.
- Add your filling ingredients.
- Fold the egg over the ingredients.
- Enjoy with Cholula.

The main ingredient (the humble egg) is the same for both. The process you choose determines the outcome.

Scrambled eggs require very little planning. The variation in outcome is based upon the amount of mixing during the cooking cycle.

Omelets require planning, decision making, preparation, patience, and finesse. They also require practice and the acceptance of potential failure.

If your omelets consistently come out scrambled, the egg isn't the problem. It's **you**.

2. The Customer Comes First!

A customer is the most important visitor on our premises. He is not dependent on us. We are dependent on him. He is not an interruption to our work. He is the purpose of it. He is not an outsider to our business. He is a part of it. We are not doing him a favour by serving him. He is doing us a favour by giving us the opportunity to do so.

-Mahatma Gandhi

They may be called patients, constituents, clients, partners, subjects, passengers, users, visitors, viewers, members, patrons, applicants, donors, or the old standby, customers. It doesn't matter what type of organization you manage; your organization has customers. Your department may not serve any of these external customers. In that case, your department (hopefully) serves internal customers who, in turn, serve external customers.

Without customers, your organization or department has no reason to exist. There's nobody to consume your great products and services. When someone comes up with an idea for a "better mousetrap" or a new product or service that solves a big, hairy problem, that really means the person has invented some product or service that lots of customers will use and, hopefully, buy.

It's no exaggeration to say that customers are the lifeblood of any organization.

As companies grow in size and complexity, they often fall into the trap of creating "customer-facing specialty departments" like customer care, help desks, customer-experience management, customer advocacy, and a whole host of other titles and departments that focus on the customer. The truth is that, as the lifeblood of the organization, every employee and every manager should be "customer-facing."

I'm not advocating the elimination of these specialty departments. I am lamenting the fact that many weak employees and managers use these customer-facing departments as a crutch or a barrier between themselves and their customers. The more an organization separates itself from its customers, the more it risks alienating and losing its customers.

It is your job, as a manager, to keep your organization close to its customers. The customers should be your primary focus. Ensuring that your customers' experience is the best it can be, every day, should be your number-one priority. Putting customers at the top of your priority list will ensure you don't lose sight of their importance. It will also help ensure that you keep your existing customers as you continue the search for new ones.

Maintaining and building the trusting relationship you have with your customers is an extremely valuable investment. Many studies have concluded that it costs between four and ten times more to acquire new customers than it does to keep an existing one. This fact alone should be a reminder of the value of your existing customers. Your customers have progressed from not knowing you or your company to trusting you enough to buy your products or services. They have added your company to their trusted ecosystem. They expect your organization to deliver value every day. They expect and deserve your organization's attention.

Never forget it.

Becoming the Chief Simplicity Officer

Can you name the most important thing that Amazon and Google have in common? You could easily say technology, marketing, or disruptive innovators.

If you said simplicity, give yourself a gold star. While they have other things in common, the one thing that makes them leaders in their fields is their simplicity. And these are anything but simple companies!

Imagine the operational complexity at Amazon as you click around its site, looking for a Kindle book to read on your next flight, an inflatable kayak for your upcoming vacation, or the Reynolds Wrap Foil your youth group needs for this weekend's snack bar.

You don't need to worry about which vendor partner or warehouse has the goods you're purchasing. The server farms that power and deliver the website to your device never enter your mind. The patchwork quilt of state and federal laws that Amazon must navigate aren't your concern. Amazon handles the logistics involved in instantaneously determining your price, shipping costs, and sales taxes. All you have to do is select the items from an easy search bar and make sure the prices are competitive (however you define the word competitive).

Navigating Amazon's online store is simple. The site even recommends accessories for your purchases. Do you need a paddle or life preserver to go with your kayak? Amazon has taken something incredibly complex and presented it to the customer in a simple way. Do you prefer to use Amazon from your mobile device? No problem, that's simple too.

Google doesn't say how many servers it has, but the number is thought to be well over a million, spread across the world in at least a dozen gigantic data centers. Google's data centers continuously consume at least 260 million watts of electricity. How's that for an electricity bill?

Google indexes over twenty billion web pages a day, and handles over three billion daily search queries. It serves up millions of YouTube videos every day to millions of viewers. Google provides millions of map queries and turn-by-turn directions to just about anywhere on the planet on a daily basis.

Want to do your search in German, Spanish, French, or any number of other languages? No problem, just enter your search in the language of your choice, and the search returns what you're looking for in that language.

I spent a few minutes googling these factoids, but, as a consumer of Google's services, I never have to know any of it. Google works tirelessly to make sure its services are easy to consume. Google's home page is a feat of simplicity. Enter the search you're interested in, and it handles the rest.

How simple is your company? To put it more succinctly, how simple is your company from your *customers' perspective*? How easy is it to access your services, to buy your products? How much expertise do your customers need in order to work with your company? How much of your company's operational complexity gets exposed to your customers?

Customers have shown time and time again that they gravitate to the simplest solutions. I've highlighted only two companies as beacons of simplicity. I could have added Apple, McDonald's, Geico, and countless others that have seen great success by making the complex simple.

Looking for ways to put customers first? Focus on becoming their Chief Simplicity Officer.

> Simplicity equals success. Complexity
> equals failure. It's that simple.

3. Employees Don't Work for You

Ask employees to list the things they "work for." I guarantee managers will not be at the top of that list, if they make the list at all. The following is generally what employees are working for:

- To earn a paycheck
- To make a living for myself and/or my family
- To experience the challenge
- To grow
- To have fun with my coworkers
- To create something bigger than myself
- To be a part of an organization that shares my values

Ironically, if you ask a lot of managers to describe their organizations, they will often tell you how many people they have working for them. Really? How is it that employees are working for a whole list of things other than managers, yet managers list how many people are working for them? How can this basic premise of the relationship between management and employees be so disconnected?

Is it just semantics to say that employees don't work for their managers; they report to their managers? Quite the contrary. It's critical for managers to realize that their employees merely report to them. Employees take direction, seek motivation, look for clarity, look for support, and often look for permission or forgiveness from their managers. But they don't work *for* their managers.

Great managers actually work *for* their employees. The managers' focus should be creating environments where their employees, and by extension, their businesses can be successful. This means that managers are, first and foremost, service providers to their employees. Managers are responsible for ensuring that any obstacles to great performance are removed from their employees' paths. These obstacles may come from outside the organization, or, as is often the case, the biggest obstacles will come from within.

What are some obstacles to great performance? It can be as simple as the climate control in the office. It may be too cold or too hot for employees to concentrate on their work. Employees may be struggling to get their jobs done with faulty or worn-out tools. How about the work environment that has an employee who disrupts the rest of the team or isn't pulling his or her weight? All of these are examples of issues managers need to be aware of. Not only that, managers need to take swift action to eliminate these barriers to performance, in service to their employees.

And that's just it, if managers are paying attention to the needs of their employees, they will be able to move quickly to help their employees succeed. After all, an employee's success is the key to the organization's success, and, in turn, the manager's success.

Theory X and Theory Y

In 1960, Douglas McGregor (a founding faculty member of MIT's Sloan School of Management), wrote *The Human Side of Enterprise*. His book changed the direction of management education for the next fifty years. It asked (and answered) one simple question: Why do people work?

McGregor contrasted two sets of assumptions about human behavior (Theory X and Theory Y).

Theory X was a prevailing theory at the time, and its assumptions included:

- The average human being has an inherent dislike of work and will avoid it if possible.
- Since people dislike work, most people must be coerced, controlled, directed, and threatened with punishment to get them to put forth adequate effort toward achieving organizational objectives.
- The average human being prefers to be directed, wishes to avoid responsibility, has relatively little ambition, and wants security above all.

He offered Theory Y as an alternative, with these assumptions:

- The expenditure of physical and mental effort in work is as natural as play or rest.
- External control and threat of punishment are not the only means of bringing about effort toward organizational goals. People will exercise self-direction and self-control in the service of objectives to which they are committed.
- Commitment to objectives is a function of the rewards associated with their achievement.
- The average human being learns, under proper conditions, not only to accept but to seek responsibility.

- The capacity to exercise a relatively high degree of imagination, ingenuity, and creativity in the solution of organizational problems is widely, not narrowly, distributed in the population.
- Under the conditions of modern industrial life, the intellectual potential of the average human being is only partly utilized.
- Unleashing each employee's intellectual and creative energy will result in huge contributions toward the organization's success.

Theory Y acknowledges and harnesses the power of the employee. Power that can be multiplied many times over by a manager who focuses on creating an environment that maximizes the intellectual and creative potential of each employee.

4. Maintain Two Standard Deviations

I had lots of statistics classes in college. We learned a ton of formulas for measuring things like economic order quantity, measuring cycle times, and the differences between mean, median, mode, and midrange. We learned how to calculate the probability of certain outcomes and how various outcomes relate, or don't relate, to each other. These are all great, and each has its place.

One of my operations management classes (which came after finishing the statistics prerequisites) showed us a nice set of measurements and formulas for determining if something is "in control" or not. Funny thing is, I don't remember the actual formulas, but I definitely remember the lessons.

If you take a series of measurements of something like cycle time (the time it takes to produce a widget, for example), you can plot these measurements on a graph. By calculating the average (which might actually be the mean, midrange, or mode—I can't remember), you can then derive the standard deviation. If your cycle-time measurements in this example are all within two standard deviations of the average, then your system is, by definition, "in control."

I've probably botched it in terms of the statistics, and that isn't the important thing here. The key lesson is that everything you do as a manager should be within two standard deviations. The standard-deviation measurement is a metaphor for your behavior, your reactions to good and bad news, your response to competitive threats, and the way you conduct your life in general. By maintaining two standard deviations, people around you can rely upon that aspect of your character. They need to know, and rely upon knowing, that you will be measured in your response, your feedback, and your approach to business issues.

This means that you won't be the type of manager who storms around the office, yelling at people when bad news arrives. You're also not the person who runs around whooping it up and hugging everyone when good news comes your way. When a competitor makes a move that potentially damages your organization, you will exercise restraint in your emotional response.

Does this mean you become a robot? I sometimes say that I am a robot in a work setting, but I am joking when I say it. As a manager, you are by no means a robot. You can be happy, sad, angry, afraid, sick, and tired, or any other range of emotions. But you are the one in control of each of these emotions.

The two-standard-deviations rule provides a lot of leeway in your behavior, both positive and negative. You will become a more subtle and thoughtful operator if you keep two standard deviations in mind as you move through your day and your career.

Those who work with you, report to you, and rely on you will appreciate this two-standard-deviations philosophy. Volatility in a work setting stifles creativity. Who will take the risk of being creative when his or her manager is a powder keg, waiting to blow up at the first sign of a mistake? Creativity breeds innovation but also carries the risk of failure. A failure that no employee will risk if his or her manager's response to failure is to blow up and start yelling.

Such an environment also stops the flow of honest and accurate information. Employees will adjust the flow of information to a volatile manager in an attempt to yield a positive response. The content of the information becomes secondary. The delivery becomes the primary concern for the employee. This leads to information being skewed, manipulated, or shielded from the unreasonable manager. Without an accurate information flow, decisions and strategies will not be as effective, and may be wrong altogether.

Employees take on the style and demeanor of their managers. Not just their direct managers, but all the way up the chain of management to the top of their organizations. While this adoption isn't 100 percent, obviously, the adoption is quite evident.

A volatile or out-of-control manager will have an employee base that is similarly volatile. An environment that lacks trust will develop. Trust is the bedrock of any team. Without an environment of trust, the multiplying power of the strong team is eliminated. Without trust, working across organizational boundaries is nearly impossible. The organization becomes a group of disconnected islands, often lobbing shells at each other, instead of focusing on delivering results for the organization.

One hundred people who are working separately will never lift a thousand-pound boulder, but one hundred people working together and trusting each other will be able to lift it. Maintaining two standard deviations in your approach to management will lead to honest and accurate flows of information, promote a trusting environment, and leverage the power of a strong team of employees. Harnessing this power is the key to management success and the success of your organization.

Moving a Boulder

The boulder was huge. By all estimates, it weighed at least twenty tons. It had rolled down the mountain and was blocking the main road into town. Various city departments sent their top managers out to assess the situation. All came back with the same assessment: the boulder was huge, and there was no way their department could move it off the road.

The road department recommended that it build a new road to go around the boulder. Given the urgency of the situation, it seemed the best option. The crews worked around the clock to build the new road. Within four weeks, they had successfully rerouted the road around the boulder. The road department was hailed for its work and sacrifice in helping the city avert the crisis brought about by the boulder.

Success? Not really.

Sure, the city attacked the problem with its best minds. It came up with a novel approach to solving the problem. The road department employees put in a heroic effort to reopen the vital artery into the city.

But something was missing (other than jackhammers and tractors). The most vital ingredients to problem solving were missing from the story. Those ingredients are trust and teamwork.

Each manager sought a solution from within the artificial boundaries of his or her own department and experience. Each one's assessment was correct, from his or her limited perspective. None had the resources to move the boulder. Each fell victim to, and tacitly supported, a culture that ignores (and avoids) cross-departmental teamwork.

Imagine what might have happened if even two of the departments trusted each other. Imagine if they had found a way to pool their resources and ideas. By working together, they could have found a way to move that huge boulder. The power of teamwork lies not only in having more hands to do the work but also in broadening the array of available solutions.

How does your organization deal with boulders blocking the road? What are you doing to change it?

5. Deliver Results

The manager's job is to deliver results. Period.

This applies to a sole proprietor and the CEO of a multibillion-dollar company. It applies to all organizations, whether nonprofit or for-profit. Results are the yardstick that measures every organization's performance and, by extension, every manager's performance.

On a macro level, results for an organization are generally stated in financial terms, relating to the rocket fuel of any organization … money. Does the organization have enough money to fulfill its mission? Financial missions vary. One mission may be to return maximum profitability and value to shareholders, and another may be to raise enough donations to provide clean drinking water to people in Africa.

Ultimately, the financial mission will drive what should be measured.

Every manager, every supervisor, every director, and so on, is responsible for meeting the financial goals of his or her organization (profits, donations, etc.). Some managers have *direct* responsibility for the financial goals, and others have *indirect* responsibility. At a minimum, every measurement across the organization should be a piece of the financial-goal pyramid, where performance is the foundation—as shown in the fancy graphic below:

If a department's work doesn't positively support the overall organization's financial mission or enable others to positively support that mission, it should be eliminated. This may seem ruthless, but it's not. It's about delivering results, and, in most organizations, results are financially driven. Anything not contributing (directly or indirectly) to delivering on the mission is merely a drag on the organization's performance.

It's up to you, as a manager, to determine the measurement criteria for the organization you manage. Here are some key questions to consider in determining what to measure:

- What constitutes success for your department or organization?
- How does that relate to the success of the overall organization?
- What steps are required to capture the measurements?
- Can measurements be captured without disrupting what your organization does?
- Are these measurements adequately telling the story and providing enough intelligence for you and your team to make decisions about how to improve?
- Is now the time to challenge or modify what's being measured and how it's being measured?
- Do these measurements provide your manager with the information he or she needs to make effective decisions?

The list of possible nonfinancial measurements will vary dramatically, depending on the type of organization. But here's a list of a few that might apply to your organization:

- Turnaround Time
- Cycle Time
- Uptime
- Percentage of Defects
- Unplanned Downtime
- Response Time
- Outbound Calls

- Media Impressions
- First-Call Resolution Percentage
- Packages Shipped/Received
- Customers Served
- Customer Satisfaction
- Net Promoter Score

Financial measurements have less variability across organizations but can also be quite exhaustive. Here are some to consider:

- Revenue (or Donations)
- Revenue Growth
- Cost per Acquisition (of Customers)
- Gross Margin
- Profitability
- Profitability Growth
- Net Operating Profit
- EBITDA (Earnings before Interest, Taxes, Depreciation, and Amortization)
- Budgeted versus Actuals (of Every Measure)

The mere act of measuring affects results. This was the unexpected result of experiments at the Hawthorne Works of Western Electric, in Chicago, in 1924. The original hypothesis was that productivity increases with brighter lights in the factory. That proved true. But, when they reduced the brightness, productivity improved again. With each successive increase or decrease in lighting, productivity improved. When employees knew their output levels were being measured, they found ways to continue to improve their productivity.

There is a related downside. While the things being measured are improving, other unmeasured parts of your organization may not be improving or, worse, are being sacrificed. With this in mind, don't be afraid to mix things up, measure new parts of your organization, modify parameters, and create new higher standards from time to time. The objective is the results, not the measurement process.

Managers can't be everywhere or be involved in every detail of their groups' activities. Finding measuring tools that help you understand the output of your group is critical. Depending upon the type of process you manage, these measurements may need to be reported every minute, hour, day, week, or month ... or all of the above.

We've already talked about the importance of managers serving their employees. That critical part of the process delivers results. The environment that a manager creates has to be one focused ultimately on delivering the desired results to an organization. Your measurements should focus your employees and your entire organization on delivering results. Your organization's success depends on it. Period.

Chasing Mice

Which one do you spend more time chasing ... mice or elephants?

Of course, I'm speaking metaphorically. Mice represent the small details, interesting diversions from the real questions, symptoms instead of root causes, etc. Elephants are the big strategic decisions, the tough questions, the root causes.

When budgeting for expenses (whether at home or at work), do you spend a lot of time comparing the cost of paper clips between two vendors? Do you worry about the cost of an additional travel day associated with attending a trade show or the strategic benefit of attending the show in the first place?

Do you worry about the cost differences for toner and paper or consider ways to modify your processes and eliminate the use of paper-based documents?

How often have you been in a disagreement with a friend, relative, colleague, or spouse over a "mouse" issue, and let that disagreement mask one or more "elephant" issues? The mouse issue may seem worthy of all the effort but rarely is.

Chasing mice while the elephants run free is almost always a bad idea. It wastes energy and our most important commodity, time.

Better to chase more elephants.

6. Don't Ride Your Fender!

I learned this phrase from motorcycling. It refers to a rider who always sees his fender. To see his fender, the "fender-rider" isn't looking ahead but focusing directly in front of the bike.

We could always tell if someone was riding his fender. We'd see the tilt in his head as he rode. He was looking in front of his bike, and his fender was always in his view. Think about that. How could the rider prepare for what was coming? What was his big-picture view? The next rock?

I remember riding with a about six or seven guys. My brother was in the lead, and I was somewhere near the back. We had all stopped to wait for the last in our group. There we were, sitting on our bikes, goggles off, resting and waiting. A few minutes later, here comes our last guy, standing up, head cocked down, looking at his fender. He never saw us, even though we were only about fifty feet off the trail. He went by, riding his heart out, and going quite slow. We all laughed. I've never forgotten how invisible we were, just fifty feet off the trail.

You're probably saying, "Hey, Bob, that's great, but I'm not an off-roader." Well, I don't ride motorcycles nowadays either, so I have another way to illustrate the concept. Imagine driving down the freeway while looking just a few feet in front of your car, or, better yet, looking out your side window. Amazing how fast things are whizzing past, isn't it!

Imagine if you had to make all of your driving decisions as things were whizzing past, making last-second corrections to avoid a collision, slamming on your brakes to avoid hitting a stopped car in your lane, swerving at the last second to make it to your exit. Sounds crazy, but this is exactly how some managers (and employees) operate.

Here's a business context. Do you know people who are always super busy, careening from one crisis to the next? They move at breakneck speed, almost breathless. These folks often work late, just to keep up with their workloads. Stress is a way of life for them.

When you ask them how things are going, their first responses are usually, "Busy!" They measure their days by how many fires they fought, how few minutes they had to themselves. Their days, their weeks, their years—sometimes their entire careers—fly by. Chances are these people are riding their fenders.

It's possible to appear effective while riding your fender. Fender-riders may even curry favor with their managers. Some managers will see fender-riders as great workers and dedicated employees, since they're so wrapped up in their work. Managers may also be fender-riders. That's a recipe for disaster. If managers happen to also be fender-riders, their perception of what is effective will be skewed and inaccurate. What appears to be effectiveness will ultimately show itself to be haphazard and reactive only.

I've noticed a funny thing about fender-riders. They're usually very stressed, not only at work but also in their personal lives. They are probably fender-riders at home as well. They often don't advance in their career paths (whatever those paths may be) as quickly as their non-fender-riding counterparts. Why?

First of all, how *can* they advance or take on more responsibility? They are already at their wit's end to keep up with what they're doing today. Another reason is that their lack of longer-range perspective makes their decisions over the long haul a lot less effective. They don't have the time to think about alternatives. They take the first alternative that presents itself in most any decision situation, which isn't always the best. And, because they can't see certain things coming until they are right on top of them, major potholes or obstacles for the organization aren't avoided.

With longer-range perspective, just like in a car or off-road motorcycle, you can make slight corrections to the course and avoid big obstacles. If you're looking out a few months (maybe even a year) in your business planning, rather than just the end of the month, or the next ninety days, you can make minor adjustments now that pay off a year from now, two years from now. Maybe you can avoid laying off ten people next year by seeing a slowdown coming and allowing headcount to drop by attrition, starting today.

How is it that some people are able to get their work done without being frantic? Yet others are in reaction mode, on the defensive, always tense for the next challenges they may face. You can't see if their heads are cocked in the down position, but you can see the results of fender-riders.

Avoid riding your fender, and help your employees avoid the same mistake. Look past your fender. Take in the long view. It is safer and much more effective.

Avoiding Rocks

Riding motorcycles can be dangerous. Especially when riding through a rocky section of trail.

When I rode motorcycles (a long time ago), I was always amazed at the way certain riders were able to go through rocky sections so quickly, while others struggled just to survive.

Ask anyone who can fly through rocky sections how he or she does it, and you will usually get this answer:

Focus on where you want to go, and don't look at the rocks.

An amazing thing happens if you focus on the rocks. You inevitably run into them.

The same thing happens with potholes. The surest way to hit a pothole is to focus on it.

We all have rocks (or potholes) in our paths. They will always be there. The best way to avoid them is to resist the temptation to look.

7. The Best Managers Are Curious

Curiosity may have killed the cat, but it makes a great manager. Exercising curiosity forces a manager (or anyone) to approach situations as a learner. Being curious is the opposite of thinking you know everything.

The Industrial Revolution ushered in a tremendous expansion of business enterprises, mostly in manufacturing and mass production. As thousands of new employees began working in large factories, managers were challenged with finding effective methods for managing their large enterprises. At that time, the single best example of a large organization was the US Army.

Armed forces throughout history have been top-down, command-and-control, organizational structures. Ideas and commands flow from the top of the organization, and there is little left to interpretation for those down the chain of command. Managers, in this context, are commanders, facilitating the communication and execution of orders. There is little room for questions or creativity.

This concept was effective in the context of a large, assembly-line manufacturing organization. Even in that setting, the lack of discussion, questioning, and creativity prevented employees from taking emotional ownership of their jobs. It stifled innovation.

Organizations that create an environment supporting both top-down and bottom-up communication see significantly better results. Employees and middle-level managers who "own" their processes and the outcomes of their organizations are more engaged, more creative, and much happier. Organizations with empowered and engaged employees will almost always outperform their less empowered and less engaged competition.

A curious manager asks questions, even if she thinks she knows the answer. By answering the manager's question, the employee owns the answer and the thought process that created it. The best tools for the curious manager are (obviously) questions. Managers who outline and punctuate their discussions with questions will uncover much more information than those who focus on lecturing to, or commanding, anyone who will listen.

Knowing that the manager will be asking these tough, open-ended questions will motivate the employee to consider alternatives, think about the best options, and prepare to recommend the best possible answers to the manager's questions.

Questions lead to employee empowerment and continuous process improvement. Here are some empowering questions that a curious manager can ask:

- What approach are you planning to take to handle this situation?
- What will our customers' experience be (they always come first)?
- Have you thought about any other approaches?
- Why is this approach better than any other approach?
- What did your team think about this approach?
- What will you do the next time this situation arises?
- Can we learn anything from this that we can use to be better next time?

Each question has the effect of placing ownership of the planning, its execution, and the outcome squarely on the person answering the question. This promotes keen focus and creates an environment of critical thinking. Never forget, although the employee has ownership, you continue to be accountable and responsible for the outcome of that employee's plan. It is your job to ask the questions and provide the feedback needed to help create the best potential for success.

Curiosity goes beyond a manager's interactions within the organization. It extends outside the organization. Focusing your curiosity directly on your customers and potential customers will yield great returns. How are your customers using your products and services? Why are they using them? How does it make them more successful? What are they worried about? What do they see in their future, and how is your organization going to be a part of that future? How can you help them get to their future faster?

Notice that these questions have very little to do with how much money you can make from your customers. They don't define what it will take for them to buy more of what you are offering. Those are fender-rider questions. You are thinking long-term and focusing on your customers' view of the future. Genuine curiosity, coupled with a willingness to act in the interest of your customers, will make your organization much more valuable in the long-term, rather than merely trying to create some type of short-term buying decision.

One of the Most Powerful Words in Our Vocabulary: Why?

In the hands of a toddler, it can become one of the most challenging. I remember a number of conversations with my daughters when they were in that two- to five-year-old range. They demanded the most thorough explanations of just about everything imaginable. I know that my wife and I heard "Why" at least a hundred times a day.

Why is it so powerful? Why do toddlers use it so much? Simple. It opens our minds to new information. It drives learning. It fuels the fire of curiosity that burns within each of us.

An interesting thing happens to children as they move through elementary, middle, and then high school. They are asked to provide lots of answers. What is the square root of eighty-one? What's the capital of North Dakota? What position do you play on the soccer team? What differentiates plant cells from animal cells? What are you going to be when you grow up?

This continues in college. Students take a roster of classes for a semester (or quarter). They display their mastery by providing the correct answers to questions on a series of midterm and final exams. Understanding the "why" of something is less important than getting the correct answer.

We're told that there are no dumb questions ... only those that aren't asked. After a lifetime of answering mundane questions from others, is it any wonder that many people have fallen out of practice, or are afraid, when it comes to asking real questions?

Are you using "Why?" as much today as you did when you were younger?

Is the fire of curiosity still burning for you?

Why not?

8. Always Cultivate Talent

There are very few truly one-man (or one-woman) shops. Show me a successful sole proprietor, and I'll show you someone who leads and relies upon a team of talented individuals ... whether that person realizes it or not.

How can this be? Doesn't the definition of sole proprietor mean that one person is the sole talent that makes everything happen? Not quite.

Imagine that you're an awesome flower arranger. Your bouquets are exquisite. Their beauty is unmatched. You decide to take a risk and open your own flower shop. Your confidence is high. After all, your flower arrangements are incredible. Customers will come from miles around to buy your arrangements.

A few weeks into the process of opening your new shop, you discover that flower shops don't run on flower arrangements alone. There are building leases to negotiate, furniture and fixtures to procure, point-of-sale systems to deploy, website interfaces to create (if you'd like to receive orders from the national flower delivery services). You have suppliers to line up and insurance coverage to purchase. You need merchant account services (if you plan to take credit cards) and payroll systems (for the one or two part-time employees you'll be hiring, just for starters).

You'll need to connect your talent with the talents of a wide array of other people, just to open your shop. Once the shop makes it past opening day, you will continue to rely heavily on the talents of others to remain open and thrive.

It's the same thing in a larger company. Your ability to build trusting relationships across your company and across your industry will have more to do with your long-term success than your individual talent. Creating a reservoir of trust with talented people, and relying on them, just as you'd rely on yourself, is critical to your success … and theirs.

Management is not only a people business. It's also a talent business. Finding, mixing, and matching the right talent, at the right time, to achieve your organization's success is a fundamental part of your job. How do you meet this talent challenge? Always cultivate talent.

Each of your direct reports is part of your talent pool. Each has specific strengths and weaknesses. How can you capitalize on his or her strengths while determining the best route to eliminate his or her weaknesses? The answer will vary for each employee. The process starts with candid discussions with each employee about ways to improve his or her talent level. What are his or her interests, and is he or she willing to own the process of improving his or her talent? On-the-job skills training, books (like this one), off-site or on-line classes, college courses, and departmental learn-at-lunch programs are all potential resources you might provide to your employees.

Talent is all around you. Employees in other departments, competing companies, friends of friends, students on college campuses, bloggers and consultants, and just about every other person outside of your organization, may be candidates to join your organization in the future. The homework you've done scouting and cultivating relationships across and outside your organization will pay huge dividends when it's time to add new talent.

Your talent, alone, won't be enough. Enough for what? Enough to accomplish whatever the definition of success is for you, your department, or your company.

The Kung Fu Master

"The measure of a Kung Fu Master isn't his own Kung Fu, but that of his student..." -Author Unknown

There are many measures of greatness in life: wealth, fame, popularity, just to name a few. These pale by comparison to the positive impact we can and should have on others.

Look around you. Who are your students? Do you take the time to teach? Are you an example for your students? Are you helping others achieve their greatness and celebrating when they do?

We don't have much time on this planet. Our energy, our ideas, and the passion we have for our ideas can live on in our students ... and their students.

Imagine if each of us were measured like the Kung Fu Master. The truth is that we are, whether we know it or not.

9. Don't Treat Everyone the Same

Each of us is unique, just like everyone else.

Each of us works for our own unique reasons. We each have unique interests, skill sets, passions, goals, strengths, and motivations. We each have our own fears, phobias, preconceived ideas, mental blocks, sensitivities, personal battles, and weaknesses.

Knowing that each person is unique, it stands to reason that your employees will be unique and require different types of management intervention. Something that motivates one employee to perform beyond his or her limits may have exactly the opposite effect on another employee.

Before I go much further, I need to throw out this "legal" disclaimer. Treating employees differently doesn't mean that managers should discriminate, play favorites, play one employee against another, or do anything else that isn't, at all times, fair and just to their employees.

And that's just it. Fairness and equitability for employees often gets boiled down in organizations to mean that each employee should receive the exact same experience when dealing with managers. After all, *fairness* is the key. While this is true on the surface, providing the exact same experience to each employee will result in abject failure for the organization.

Here's the tricky part for you, as the manager. You have to walk the line of fairness and equitability while, at the same time, understanding the unique needs of each of your direct reports. You need to know your direct reports well enough to know what motivates *them* to perform at *their* best.

What are their hot-button issues? What do they want from their manager? Do they want or require lots of direction? Do they like autonomy? Do they like the status quo? Do they like rapid change? Where do they want to go? What do they want to learn? What are their strengths? Weaknesses? Do they want to know about their weaknesses? Do they want to avoid their weaknesses or tackle them head on and turn them into strengths?

One constant in nature is that nothing is constant. How is each of your employees changing over time? The answers to each of these questions will differ for each of your employees (and yourself). The answers will point the way to how you should treat each of your employees so they maximize their value to themselves and the organization.

Encouraging Words

When talking to your friends, family, employees, or anyone else, do you use encouraging words or discouraging words?

The words and tone you choose matter. They reflect and impact your attitude. Your words are the window into your perspective on the world.

Choose discouraging words, and you actively create a discouraging environment for those around you.

Choose encouraging words, use encouraging questions, and guess what … you create an encouraging environment.

The power to create an encouraging environment, an encouraging attitude, is in your hands every day.

Here's an exercise for you. Seek out three people to encourage today. Encourage them with your words, your questions, and your actions. Show them that you are genuinely interested in what they have to say. Be appreciative of their unique efforts and skills. Actively consider how to help them be more successful in achieving their goals. Repeat this exercise every day.

Does this exercise make you uncomfortable? If so, maybe you should be the first person you seek out to encourage.

10. Never Stop Learning (or Teaching)

I don't know who said, "No man is an island." I can guess at the original intent of this quote. But my application of this quote in the business world takes on a few dimensions. First, it means that no matter how confident you are in what you're doing today, the world around you never stops changing. That thing you are confident about today may be obsolete tomorrow.

Competitors are always looking for ways to gain an advantage against your company, no matter what product or service you deliver. These competing forces may be next door, across town, or on the other side of the globe … but they are there.

How do you remain competitive? Never stop learning. Learn and embrace new ideas, innovations, new pricing models, and new delivery pathways. Get to know all the players in your field. Who are they, what are they doing, why are they doing what they're doing?

Who are your competitors? What do they do differently from you? Why do customers like your competitors? Who are the thought leaders and influencers within your industry and your customer base? Why are they the influencers? Who do they know? Where do they get their advice? What would it take for you to become an influencer?

Don't let an "island mentality" stop you from connecting with others. Actively participate and understand the ecosystem of the industry or industries where your organization operates. Who are the suppliers to your industry? Who's doing things right? Who's going in the wrong direction? Who are the people you'd like to hire for your organization if the opportunity arises?

What are other industries doing? You may be surprised to learn that some of your best innovations and ideas will come from studying what other industries are doing. You can learn lessons in lots of strange places. Be on the lookout for them.

Thriving businesses don't just maintain their competitive advantages. They extend their advantages, compete in new markets, grow their franchises, and create new ones. If you choose to ignore the churn of new ideas, changing customer preferences, and the ever-evolving and changing societal structures across the world, you do so at your own peril. The world around you will evolve and change, whether you choose to participate or not.

Learning isn't just a book thing. You've chosen to read this book. I applaud your decision! Learning is an investment of your time and energy in finding new ideas and new perspectives. Constant learning is a mind-set. It feeds your curiosity and leads to greater understanding. Through constant learning, you will ask better questions of yourself and those around you.

Constant learning means staying in touch with all aspects of the marketplace. What are the new trends? Where is your industry going in the next three to five years? Is your organization influencing the new directions, or are you only reacting and responding to what other organizations are doing? How are you positioned? Are you on offense or defense?

What are the laws or other regulatory pressures that impact your industry and your organization in particular? Make it your business to understand these regulations for yourself. It's okay to rely on others to spend 100 percent of their time involved in these types of questions (lawyers, accountants, etc.), but you need to be completely familiar with your legal environment as well. The decisions you make will have legal ramifications for your organization.

Find the text of the laws that impact your organization, read articles by others that analyze or comment on the regulations. Talk to lawyers, your own legal counsel, others who may have insights. It doesn't matter what your field is. There is at least one set of legal or regulatory frameworks that impact your product or service. Often more than one framework will govern your organization, especially if your business operates in multiple jurisdictions, counties, states, or countries.

By now, you may be saying, "Hey, all of this learning is great. Sharpening my skills will make me a better manager. Getting to know my industry is a good idea. But I'm just a department supervisor. I'm not responsible for knowing this much about the whole industry. My job is to deliver results in my department. That's what I get paid to do."

You are just as much of a participant in your industry as your CEO is. For lack of a better term, you are the only CEO of your career path. Your curiosity and depth of knowledge in your chosen field will determine how much you thrive in your career. When you invest in yourself by continuously learning, those around you will see your example.

Your organization will invest in you. After all, why should it invest in you if you aren't investing in yourself? Your value starts with you, and you only become more valuable if you constantly challenge yourself to learn, adapt, innovate, and create. This means asking questions that no one else is asking—connecting in ways no one else is connecting.

The flip side of learning is teaching. Find a way to teach others everything you learn in all areas. This doesn't mean that you should prepare a lecture for every employee interaction, but it does mean that every encounter is an opportunity to both learn and coach. The little secret about teaching is that the teacher learns more than the student does. Learning enough about a topic to then teach it to others is an investment that will pay back many times over.

What new skills do your employees need? Are training opportunities available that will make them more valuable to the organization? Connect your employees with new opportunities to learn. Provide skills training. Ask crazy questions to pique their curiosity. Find the employees who are seeking new skills, and help them. These curious employees are your organization's future.

Success of those around you, those who report to you, and those you report to should always be your goal. There is no such thing as job security by holding on to your unique skills or the unique nature of your particular position. If you hold on too tightly to your job, guess what, you will get to keep it forever—or at least until the world figures out a better way to deliver what you deliver. Obsolescence should be a powerful motivator for you to keep learning, keep innovating, and continuously teach those around you.

The real power of learning and teaching is the culture of curiosity and creativity that it fosters. The more people within your organization who take learning and teaching seriously, the stronger your organization will be. Numerous management texts explain the "multiplier effect" of management. The idea is that one manager's value to an organization is multiplied, sometimes exponentially, if that manager can leverage the power of each direct report to produce great work. Constant learning and teaching are the most effective ways to ignite the multiplier effect within your organization.

Think like a Teacher ...

You're sitting in a training class. The instructor is describing a new set of management concepts or the latest system enhancements. You try to listen and stay focused. Your mind wanders a bit. You force it back in line. After all, there may be something useful you can apply to your work.

Later, someone asks you how the class went. You shrug your shoulders, reporting that you learned a couple of new things. You then have trouble describing what you've learned. Not an inspiring endorsement.

Imagine the same training class. But now you're there to learn the material well enough to present the same class to another group next week.

You don't get to pick and choose what applies to your work. You need to learn the subject in its entirety. Preparing to teach a subject requires active learning. You'll watch how the material is presented, the visual aids and examples the presenter uses, and the way the presenter moves around the room. Nothing less than full mastery of the information will suffice. Anything less could lead to failure when it's your turn to teach.

Do yourself a favor. Prepare like a teacher, learn like a teacher, and think like a teacher. The truth is you will be teaching this class next week—to yourself—as you try to remember and apply what you learned in the class.

11. Match Authority with Responsibility

It was an interesting call. My friend called and said, "Hey, Bob. What do you know about the notary business? We just fired the guy in charge of our notary business, and I recommended you to Ted (his boss). I gave him your number. Expect his call."

I didn't have time to respond to the question. My call waiting beeped, and it was Ted calling. "Hi, Bob. You come highly recommended. We have this notary business here, and things aren't going very well, so I've had to make a change. I'm told you are just the guy we need to come in and turn this business around for us. Can you come in for an interview to discuss the opportunity?"

Had I responded to my friend's question, I would have said that I knew nothing about the traveling notary business. I had a background managing various operations but no experience managing a nationwide notary business. Let alone one that was performing so poorly that the last guy in charge was fired.

Before I knew it, I was in my interview. Ted gave me a quick description of the high points of the notary business. I liked him, I liked the larger organization I'd be joining, and I knew from my friend that the culture of this company matched well with my personality. Everything fit, and about twenty-four hours later, I had accepted Ted's offer. A few days later, I was in my new job, turning around a fledgling, nationwide traveling notary business.

Why am I telling this story? To provide context for what happened when I arrived on my first day.

The phone rang, and it was Ted (his office was in another building, across town). "Hey, Bob. Welcome aboard! I'm glad you were able to find the place and your new office. Sorry I can't be there in person

Leadership Starts (and ends) in Your Head

to welcome you to the company. The main supervisor in your group is Christie, so you should start things by talking with her. I think you'll know what your next steps are after that. Let's plan to get together in a couple of weeks, and you can update me on what you've learned and what you're doing to move things in the right direction. Bob, I'm pleased to have you on board running this business. Talk to you later."

That was it. He "introduced" me to one person. The rest was up to me. He was confident that I'd find and meet my new team, study and become an expert on the traveling notary business, learn about the existing operational processes, meet with our sales team, meet with our customers (did we have any customers?), do whatever it took to start turning the ship around, *and* be prepared for our update meeting in a couple of weeks.

Ted had given me the authority to do what I thought was right. He wasn't going to hover over me, asking for updates every day. And he knew that the best way to move my frame of mind from being the new guy to being the guy who owned this business was to hand me the keys and step back.

I'd be operating autonomously, making it up as I went. I knew that if I didn't take concrete steps to turn this business around, I'd be held responsible in much the same way as my predecessor. In one phone call, Ted matched my level of authority with my level of responsibility. After one call, I had *emotional ownership* of my new role. I owned this business, and he expected me to turn it around. All by 8:15 a.m. on my first day. Masterful.

Ted worked within his own set of time, attention, authority, and responsibility constraints. He had numerous business units reporting to him, and mine was the smallest one (of course, I planned to change that). He had his own authority to hire and fire, to set strategic priorities, to establish financial targets, and to work with customers. He didn't have the time or attention span to dig into the operational details of each of the businesses he managed on a daily basis. Just like me, he was responsible for the performance of the vast array of business units that he managed. His authority matched his responsibility.

Authority and responsibility are related but vastly different. Authority refers to the manager's ability to make autonomous decisions. A shorthand word for responsibility is blame. Who gets blamed if something doesn't work or perform as expected?

If a manager has authority to operate and make decisions in a particular part of the organization, and is held responsible for only the results from those areas of operation, that manager's authority matches his or her responsibility. If the manager is held responsible for personal performance and for areas of the organization beyond the areas where that manager has authority to act, then that manager's authority and responsibility are not matching.

Matching authority and responsibility is critical. A manager whose responsibility is wider than his or her authority will quickly become frustrated. The manager's stress level will climb. His or her patience will be tested regularly. Emotional ownership in this mismatched environment is impossible. A manager needs to own the whole thing or nothing. There is no half-ownership, no "sort of pregnant." If a manager doesn't have full ownership, then that manager won't own it emotionally. The chances of success drop dramatically. Processes, departments, and entire organizations that aren't "owned" often fail mysteriously. Everyone works hard, yet it fails. Nobody owned it, so nobody had a sense of personal success or failure tied to it.

A mismatched authority and responsibility environment leads to disengagement and hopelessness for just about everyone involved—managers and employees. The negative effects of this type of dysfunctional environment are far-reaching. Successes are often by accident and hard to systematically repeat.

As organizations grow and change, areas of authority and responsibility will grow and change as well. Keep this balance in mind as you participate in this growth. Achieving equilibrium between authority and responsibility is a foundational task for each manager at every level of the organization.

No One Is "Just a …"

"I don't know the answer. I'm just a temp."

"I can't authorize that refund. I'm just a cashier."

"Clearly, nobody here cares what I think. I'm just a worker bee."

"I could probably help those wounded veterans, but I'm just a private citizen. I'm sure there's a government agency for that."

"There's no way I could ever do that job. I'm just a high school graduate."

Listen closely, and you'll hear the "I'm just a …" phrase applied in many circumstances. You may even use it yourself. I've inflicted it on myself a time or two (or three).

Ownership is risky. It requires personal responsibility, a willingness to step up, the ability to make hard choices, and being accountable for your actions. "I'm just a …" is a ticket to minimizing the expectations we place on ourselves.

The Dark Side

"Just a …" has an even darker side. We can use it to limit the expectations we place on those around us:

"John's a decent manager, but he's really just a guy keeping the trains coming in on time. I doubt he could step into anything new."

"She's just a summer intern, so I don't expect her to light the world on fire for us."

"He's just a beginner, so we need to cut him some slack."

"She's just a kid."

"He's just a drug addict, so he will never amount to much."

When expectations are minimized, minimized outcomes usually follow.

Applying the "just a …" phrase to anyone, including ourselves, ignores potential. It ignores our ability to take ownership, grow, change, improve, and amaze.

12. Visualize Success

Watch athletes before an event ... pole vaulters, golfers, snowboarders, ice skaters, motocross racers, rugby players, batters in a batter's box. What are they thinking about? They are definitely not thinking about failure. They're visualizing how to be successful. They are visualizing success and what it looks like. They are preparing their minds and bodies to produce that success. If you see the success, you can create it. If you see failure, you will create it.

Talk to golfers, whether PGA pros or weekend warriors. They never like to hear negativity on the course. They are visualizing success. They push negative ideas out of their heads. The putt will go the way I want it to go. My driver will work off the tee. The lake that we are hitting over isn't a concern. What water? They're visualizing the arc of the ball in the air as it approaches its perfect landing spot on the green, rolling up within a few feet of the hole.

Does the ball behave the way we visualize every time? Maybe not. Guess what ... it will never behave the way we want it to, unless we first visualize it.

What defines success for your employees? What is their perspective on how the organization helps them be successful? Can you visualize how the organization needs to improve to make them even more successful?

What does success look like in your organization? Does it have something to do with customers? The obvious answer should be, "Yes, our success has everything to do with the customer." Customers are the reason any organization exists. It doesn't matter whether the customers are internal, external, or both. No organization should exist if it doesn't serve the needs of a customer.

Your organization should always view the definition of success through the eyes of your customers and prospective customers. How do you look to them? What makes them a raving fan today? What needs to improve to get more fans tomorrow? What do they like about your organization? What do they dislike? Visualizing from your customers' perspectives should drive the way you prioritize your organization's work.

Do you have an important meeting coming up in the near future? Take the time to imagine the setting, the people, and the topics. Who called the meeting? What's the goal of the meeting? What is every participant hoping to gain from the meeting? What are the main points you plan to bring to the meeting? These can be tough questions to answer, especially if you didn't call the meeting. Visualizing the meeting before it starts will help you answer these questions and be more effective where it counts ... in the meeting.

After the meeting, compare the reality to what you visualized. How accurate were you? What can you change to make your visualization more accurate? Better yet, what can you change within your organization to make what you visualized a reality in the next meeting?

Which would you rather have in your organization: ten employees who know how to visualize success or ten employees who are experts on what failure looks like? Obviously, the ten who visualize success. Visualizing failure is easy. Visualizing success is even easier. It's the first step toward creating success.

What about visualizing the accolades of success? That's a waste of your time. Success is its own reward. This isn't a cliché, and this can be a difficult mind-set to adopt. You will create and share in countless successes, both large and small. Some of the successes will appear small to the outside, but they will be huge for you ... and vice versa.

Know that a personal success is yours first and everyone else's after that. The reaction to your success is an echo of the actual success. Accolades are nice but hundreds of times weaker than the original success. Sort of like the moon's reflection of the sun's light … bright and pretty but nothing compared to the sun itself.

Visualizing how to avoid consequences is another waste of time. The statement, "I hope we don't fail, because I'd hate to explain that to my boss," is not an example of effective visualization. It's also no way to motivate your team. Starting with such low expectations is the surest way to create mediocre results. Imagine visualizing a hardy success instead of just having a goal of avoiding the tough conversation with your boss that comes with failure. Which one will lead to the best outcome for your organization?

It's difficult, even impossible, to be successful if you don't know what success looks like. Planting the images of success in your mind, and the minds of those you manage, provides the target for your organization. The definition of success can be elusive and change over time. The only way to "stay on its tail" is to visualize success every day, and then grab it and never let go.

Remembering to Breathe ...

Nearly all sports are the same (at least on one level). It doesn't matter if that sport is soccer, baseball, golf, archery, skeet shooting, curling, downhill skiing, long-distance running, ice skating, motorcycle racing, or competitive yodeling.

They each start with the same fundamentals:

- Relax and stay loose.
- Calm your mind.
- Visualize success.
- Bend your knees.
- Don't forget to breathe.

One could make a case that each of these fundamentals is of equal importance, but my money is on the last one. Consciously remembering to breathe puts us in the right state of mind to remember the other fundamentals.

We each face challenges on a daily basis. Some are small and some are huge (at least from our perspective). Tackle them the way athletes do:

- Relax and stay loose.
- Calm your mind.
- Visualize success.
- Bend your knees.
- **Remember to breathe!**

13. You Only Control One Thing

As much as we'd like to think we're in control of our work environment, our actual control is fleeting at best. The world is filled with infinite variables we don't control. Try this exercise:

Make a list of the things you don't own or control in your work environment. In fact, you can even expand the list to include the things outside of your work environment that you don't control. Go ahead; I'll be here when you finish your list.

How many items did you list? Chances are the list of things you don't own or control was quite long. You probably gave up listing them after writing down the first ten or fifteen items.

Now make a list of the things you do own or control. This list should only have things you completely control. These are the things that no person, place, thing, idea, or any other influencer, can impact. You are the master of the items on this list.

How many items are on that list? I submit to you that your list will have one item, no matter how long you think about it. Actually, it will have one item and a subitem. What is the one thing you fully control? Your attitude.

The good news is that your attitude is everything you need to control. You get to choose the attitude you bring to the world every day. Choosing a strong, confident, flexible, and creative attitude will lead you to great places in life and in management. Choosing to have an overwhelmed, pessimistic, hopeless, or cynical attitude toward life will bring you exactly the opposite of great things in life.

Your attitude, which leads to the way you approach your life, is the single most important choice you will make. And you get to make your choice every day. There's an old hiring rule that goes something like "hire the attitude and train the rest." If you've ever hired anyone, you know there are a ton of other rules, regulations, human resources perspectives, background checks, and so on that go into a hiring decision. While these have their place, the first rule is the most important. Hire the attitude and train the rest.

If this is the case, what attitude are you bringing to work? Is it an attitude that will get you hired? Is your attitude a beacon for those around you? Is the attitude you've chosen one that leads you to make successful decisions? If not, why not?

What is the subitem on the list of things you control, below attitude? It is your response to the things you can't control? As you observed by making the list of things out of your control, we don't control much of the world around us. All of these items are variables in an equation that continuously changes. Many of these variables will interact with you and your organization regularly: threats, opportunities—you name it. The things you don't control will present themselves every day.

The good news for you is that, if you choose the right attitude, you get to control your response.

This closely relates to the two-standard-deviations rule in an earlier chapter but takes the topic a bit deeper. Two standard deviations is more about your emotional response to the things around you. But your attitude will dictate the type of response you bring to threats and opportunities. A positive and forward-looking attitude will yield a more creative response. Ultimately, your response will be more effective for your organization.

Looking at the same situation with a negative or closed attitude will do just the opposite. A negative attitude will steer the alternatives considered in a negative direction. Responses will be defensive, less creative, and much less forward-looking. Your response will not be as effective for your organization.

You don't get to control much in life or in management. But you do get to control the most important aspect of your life: your attitude. Choose the right attitude, and you will see the impact on yourself and your work. More importantly, you will see the impact on those who report to you. Although we control our own attitudes, managers carry around a dirty little secret about attitudes. They are contagious to their direct reports. Show me a manager who brings a negative or closed-off attitude to work, and I will guarantee that the majority of that manager's direct reports will have a similarly negative attitude.

Attitudes at the top of an organization dictate that nebulous and sometimes over-used word "culture" within the organization. Countless books talk about how to create positive corporate cultures. How to leverage the power of a strong corporate culture to bring success.

Corporate culture is the manifestation of the collective attitudes that the managers and employees bring to an organization. The attitudes with the most impact on corporate culture are those of the managers. This is true of managers at all levels but starts at the top. A CEO, president, or business owner with a strong, positive, and forward-thinking attitude toward life and his or her company will push the company's culture in that positive direction. That same CEO, president, or business owner with a negative, closed off, or defensive attitude will create that type of culture within an organization.

Organizations with the most positive attitudes and, therefore, the most positive corporate cultures will almost always be more successful. The employees and managers within that successful organization will have a lot more fun and take more pride in what they do than the negative organization. Which do you prefer? Make it happen!

This list of things you control may contain only one item. But that one item has the power to drive everything else. Make the right choice. Start today!

Just Another PICNIC

I learned a new acronym recently:

>PICNIC—-Problem in chair, not in computer.

Way back in the early 90s, when one of my jobs was desktop support, I referred to the same phenomena as a nut-on-the-keyboard problem. At least 80 percent of the "computer problems" were actually human problems.

It's the same thing with Cesar Millan, the dog whisperer. Most dog problems are human problems waiting to be solved. Cesar actually spends most of his time "whispering" to dog owners. Cesar can't call his show the *Human Whisperer*, even if that's an accurate description of the service he provides. To do so would alienate the audience that he's trying to help.

The challenge with humans is that most of us would rather not admit that we are the problem. It's so much easier to blame the computer, the dog, the airline, the car, the economy, the system, traffic, evil Republicans, evil Democrats, government, society, our employees, our manager, our parents, our kids. The list of excuses is infinite.

The good news is that the solution to most of these "problems" is in the chair.

14. What Does This All Mean?

My goal with this book is to describe the mind-set and attitude of the effective leader. Proper mind-set is the foundation of everything else in leadership. Mind-set is what separates mere managers from true leaders.

Leadership is a journey, just like life. You get out of it what you put in. Are you bringing energy to the journey or taking it away? Be the person bringing energy, every chance you get.

You are here to serve your employees, and, together, you and your employees are responsible for serving customers and producing results. Be a reliable and positive resource for your employees. Always. It's that simple.

You aren't in your position to order people around, get special privileges, or obsess about what your fellow managers are doing.

The more your employees own their jobs, the more they will enjoy their jobs. The highest performing organizations have the most engaged employees. You, their manager, drive your employees' engagement. You are the one who creates the environment for high engagement and high performance.

Celebrate your employees' successes. Share their challenges. Remove obstacles. Be there for them. Always look for ways to improve the environment for their successes. Doing so is the key to your success and your organization's success.

The best leaders start by managing themselves. They manage their mind-sets and never forget their missions:

- Serve their employees, their customers, and their organizations.
- Be trusted leaders.

Searching for Awesomeness

How's your search going? Have you found the awesomeness you've been seeking?

There are a lot of awesome nouns (people, places, things) out there. A whole bunch of awesome verbs. And don't forget about all the awesome adjectives. String these together in almost infinite patterns, and you have the makings of a lot of awesomeness.

The sound of steaks sizzling on the grill, a beautiful sunset, the sparkle in others' eyes when you've taught them something they never knew, the quiet stillness of a starting line just before the starter's gun goes off, the aroma of a perfect cup of coffee as the sun comes up, the crackle of a campfire, watching your daughter roast a marshmallow to perfection.

The search for awesomeness should be an easy one. It's all around us.

Sadly, for some, finding awesomeness is impossible.

That's because they don't realize that awesomeness isn't about what's outside. It's not about what we see, touch, or hear. It isn't what we smell or taste. It isn't even about who is with us.

Our thoughts drive who we are, what we'll be, where we're going, and how we look at the world. To find and experience awesomeness, we must first open ourselves to gratitude and appreciation. Without gratitude and appreciation, all of the awesomeness in this world (and beyond) are merely nouns, verbs, and adjectives waiting to be combined.

The search for awesomeness starts and ends within each of us.

Gratitude is our compass. Appreciation is our map.

I'm grateful that you read this far, and I hope you found your reading to be a productive use of your time. I'm all about results. I'd love to hear about your results and any feedback you have on this book.

Please feel free to drop me a line at EnCurUj@gmail.com

You can also follow my *Encouragement is Personal* blog at www.EnCurUj.com.

Acknowledgments

Who should one acknowledge after writing a book about the mental aspects of leadership? I could start with every manager I've had in my career. Let's see how good my memory is: Ron Oliver, Larry Fong, Aiko Kanemoto, Joe Ney, Ron Peralta, Terry Pyle, Susan DeWaters, Bryan Wilkinson, Joe Zambataro, Greg Prachar, Don Lipschutz, Cherisse Falconer, Rick Katz, Ira Halpern, Mike Shea, Scott Roecklein, Ted Moore, Curt Caspersen, Linda Saunders, Pat McLaughlin, Larry Davidson, and Robert Karraa.

I learned a great deal from each of them … mostly good things and a few things to avoid. I'm fortunate that, in almost every case, these managers believed in my abilities and did their level best to provide an environment where I could be successful.

Thank you to every employee who has reported to me. I hope you learned at least as much from me as I learned from you.

Thank you to my reviewers and sounding boards. Jeff Turner, Brandt Williams, Pat Schultz, Eric Jones, Mike Ratermann, Dan Rockwell, Kevin Lagerwey, Bob Gourlay, and Kip Haas. The feedback and commentary I received from each of you had a huge impact on this final product. Everyone but Kip, whose honesty I appreciated when he told me, "Frankly, I don't really read this type of book, but, based on your table of contents, I'd probably read this one."

Many of my most valuable leadership lessons came from my parents and my in-laws. Thank you to my mom and dad, Bob and Nancy Dailey, for showing me how to navigate often-troubled waters while staying focused on what's important. Thank you, also, to my father- and mother-in-law, John and Diane Anderson. You welcomed me into your family, not just as the husband of your daughter but as a son.

This book would not be possible without the support of my awesome wife, Janet, of over twenty-five years. She watched me sit in my home office, typing away, making progress, procrastinating, updating, deleting, changing directions, and struggling with formats, titles, and every other detail that an author stresses over. All the while, she gave me a knowing smile … a smile that said, "I know you will finish your book, and you will be proud of it when you do." Of course, she was right.

About the Author

Bob has held executive leadership positions in start-ups and privately held companies, as well as Fortune 500 companies, over the past twenty-five years. He is a sought-after management consultant and executive coach. He enjoys trail running, mountain biking, camping, off-roading, Skyping with his two daughters and their husbands, and traveling the world with his wife, Janet. He and Janet live in Southern California.

CPSIA information can be obtained at www.ICGtesting.com
Printed in the USA
BVOW04s0027051214

377837BV00001B/5/P